IN THE HEART OF MY MIND

THE INNER JOURNEY...

BY

Glendy Jane Junius

(Daughter of Cllr. Josiah David Baryogar Junius)

Copyright 2021 -In the Heart of My Mind,
The Inner Journey

by Glendy Jane Junius

All rights reserved. No part of this publication may be reproduced, distributed, or transmitted in any form or by any means, including photocopying, recording, or other electronic or mechanical methods, without the prior written permission of the publisher, except in the case of brief quotations embodied in critical reviews and certain other noncommercial uses permitted by copyright law.

Although the author and publisher have made every effort to ensure that the information in this book was correct at press time, the author and publisher do not assume and hereby disclaim any liability to any party for any loss, damage, or disruption caused by errors or omissions, whether such errors or omissions result from negligence, accident, or any other cause.

Adherence to all applicable laws and regulations, including international, federal, state and local governing professional licensing, business practices, advertising, and all other aspects of doing business in the US, Canada or any other jurisdiction is the sole responsibility of the reader and consumer.

Neither the author nor the publisher assumes any responsibility or liability whatsoever on behalf of the consumer or reader of this material. Any perceived slight of any individual or organization is purely unintentional.

The resources in this book are provided for informational purposes only and should not be used to replace the specialized training and professional judgment of a health care or mental health care professional.

Neither the author nor the publisher can be held responsible for the use of the information provided within this book. Please always consult a trained professional before making any decision regarding treatment of yourself or others.

Dedication

This Book is dedicated to the following persons, who played significant roles at various stages of my life. These individuals have helped guide my thoughts and given me the courage I needed to face all of life's challenges.

My Grandmother

Mrs. Matilda Bolo Roberts-Deceased

My Parents

Cllr. J. David Baryogar Junius- Dadthie-Deceased

Mrs. Ethel Roberts Junius- Mama

Mr. Louis B. Roberts-Uncle

My Sisters

Ms. Jedah Davidetta Junius-Pushoe-Deceased

Mrs. Louise Reeves-Gedeo

My Brothers

Mr. Collins Teah

Mr. Emmanuel Gbedee

Mr. Charles Boimah Blake

My Children

Mrs. Nathalane Dunbar-Fairley -Nat

Ms. Denise Ekeigai Abigail Reeves-Abi

Ms. Davidyne Eseh Aphlen Reeves-Dave

Ms. Charisma Ethel Newman-Rissy

Mr. James Melchizedek Reeves-Ricco

Mr. Jabez Louis Reeves-Becco

My Confidantes

Mrs. Meyartha Cordelia Logan

Mr. Hermann Leonardo Blumenthal

Mr. Michael Ansumana Padmore

*"I am my Father's daughter,
with my
Mother's beauty"*

Table of Contents

Introduction................................... 1

Chapter One: *Barren, The Calling*......... 4

Chapter Two: *Love, The Heart of All Matters*....................................... 7

Chapter Three: *Marriage Is Not for Everyone; but it Was My Choice*............11

Chapter Four: *Divorce is the One, if You are Not*..17

Chapter Five: *Singles Are Worth More Than Doubles*...............................24

Chapter Six: *Friendships Grow You*......30

Chapter Seven: *Peace Be with You*........35

Chapter Eight: Loving Again, And Blessing God for the Truth of Life.......40

Acknowledgement............................45

About the Author: *Miss Glendy Jane Junius*..46

Introduction

On many occasions in the past, I had to visit myself, and ask many tough questions looking for answers. In some of my questions, I wanted to know who I was, what I needed to change in my life, why I allowed the things that happened to me, and when would I be at peace? I asked what I needed to do, so that I would not feel the sense of emptiness, coupled with the aches I had that would not go away. I sincerely wanted to know how I could undo this state of despair and somewhat sadness I was in. Looking around, it seemed that most people around me had similar experiences and would not be able to take on assisting me with my struggles, so I decided that the help I needed, had to come from me.

The rationale for asking these questions was needed to make me aware of myself, and to help me understand the **whys** in my life. The answers are not always what you think about, not always what you want to hear, and are not what others can tell you. The answers are almost always a result of how one feels about all that they have gone through. So, to reset my timeline, I quickly created a space where I could go and debriefed my feelings into poems and quotes of relief.

My desire to write quotes grew more and more, and I developed a passion for writing and depicting all that I had gone through to include: **My life, My other life, and My new life**.

In my quotes, I described the various stages in life, with the intent to give someone the hope and freedom needed to define oneself and how we treat ourselves. As we progress in life, we go from one stage in life to the next, taking these various stages of our lives along with our personal relationship we have with God, we focus more on the problems with us, and less on God for directions and strength.

At a certain age, we believe we are truly in love, and everything is moving perfectly, everything is fine, oh yes, and no one can tell us otherwise. But soon we fall out of love, and then we develop the hate or imaginary I don't need to have a person in my life to make me feel love. At the end of the love saga, we restart the process of loving all over again, and playing the role of, I got this. In life the trips we make are many, so many that at times, we run out of gas, we miss our turns on the road, and finally we hit restart, but we find ourselves stopping several times again on the road, until we finally find our way to a new beginning.

As you read this book, and think about each of my thoughts and quotes, I hope it helps and gives you a new meaning and reason to go about your life freely, ensuring that you make yourself the focus and centerstage.

Chapter One

Barren, The Calling

I was not called to be barren, in fact, I was not barren. Yet people call me barren and did all they could to make me feel barren, so I believed I was barren.

"The pain of bareness is never relieved without the sound of a baby."

"I was childless, but never faithless"

"A woman remains who she is despite being barren, Respect that!!!"

"I am barren, but I am not broken."

"I have aches, I have pains, I feel empty, yet I am alive."

"I hope, I had no aches or pains. I hope my tomorrow was here now. I hope my past lessons are always cherished."

"Friendship filled, empty but still fill."

"Children are gifts, but do you give up if you have none? No, you live like you do, with hope."

"Race at your own pace, yet ironically time waits for no person: man and woman."

"Motherhood will bring you joy, it will bring you pain, but there's nothing like motherhood."

"And after all is said and done, the sound of a baby crying soothes and heals, and no I am not barren after all."

Psalm 113:9

"He gives the barren woman a home, making her the joyous mother of Children. Praise the Lord."

Chapter Two

Love, The Heart of All Matters

Do we ever take a minute to decide what love is, or how we should love and when we should love? I think we should always ask and have answers for all these questions, and the last question to ask needs to be, is this thing that I feel really Love?

"Life is a gift. Cherish it. Live it well."

"Talk to yourself about yourself and be very critical of yourself when love is a focus."

"Love, It's the easiest way out, we think, but then again, it is not as easy as we think, Love requires work."

"So, I say my heart loves you, and I know this is because love depicts heart, but no one has ever seen love in a heart, so I think my heart love you."

"I Love you dearly, or rarely, whatever it is one can validate feelings, and not love."

"What is your Color?"

"Color describes a red dress."

"Black and white interprets: Dirty/Clean: differences."

"I am colorful"

"I am black"

"I am white"

"I am distinct"

"Some see only colors; others see beneath the colors. Love sees the person away from the color, and I love me in all colors, black and white."

"Never be too comfortable in your comfort zone."

"After it all, love allows the people in our surroundings to see the peace within you."

"Love should always conquer all, yet love is painful."

"Love out boldly and try not to hesitate on your happiness."

"Loving at a young age, will always have many errors, so let no age determine love."

"Is love a glass, can it break? Is the break temporary, can the break be mended? I think not."

"Love forward, and not backwards."

1 John 4:18

"There is no fear in Love. But Perfect love drives out fear because fear has to do with punishment. The one who fears is not made perfect in love."

Chapter Three

Marriage Is Not for Everyone; but it Was My Choice

Some couples should not be together, but who can say to someone who has made a choice to be married that they should not be married. When you make a choice to get married, I pray that you are also able to see the signs that let you know when it does not feel right. I am inspired by my courage to allow the inner most personal thoughts to surface in my writing of quotes. Now, it has helped me understand that marriage is a choice, and more details of this point will be discussed in books to be written in the future.

"While Walking, somehow, we met. Was it a coincidence or a meant to be? And before, the walking starts with extended hands and "no flexion, I accept the offer, and secured our space together, let us walk with our peace we found."

"Prints, never the same impression, no matter the quality. Your print is unique to you."

"How do I repair one's broken heart: I admit I wronged you, I acknowledged my faults."

"The peace one shares is different from the peace to behold, the peace one desires and have, should be explicit."

"Good enough, some would say, and others would say, you're not good enough. But to me enough means adequate, so I am just adequate."

"I love you...but do I love me...and if you love me, do you see me loving me?"

"Between two lovers, mind connections will help to sustain the relationship."

"Don't find a soul mate, find a mate that respects your soul."

"A partner must compliment you. Must have your interest. Must share your ideas. Must be your company."

"Regrets,

I regret this, I regret that I wish I knew then what I know now.

How can you regret what's in the past, it's done and can't be changed so what's the reason for the regrets? I had no regrets then, and none now?

So, if I was happy then, why am I sad now? Regrets are for the future not the past."

"I found my tongue and became bold,

I hated asking for things I wanted, and it hurt to want things badly and not ask or get them...

I was determined to say how I felt, how you made me feel directly, what could be done to make me feel better, and what I saw and wanted....

I found my tongue and let my tears go... I became bold, bold enough to be direct and get the treatment I deserved; my boldness helped define me."

"And Our Resolve is,

We have agreed it is all we got

No matter the degree of aches and pains

There are scars, some we still nurse daily

Our resolve

Will pierce the unopened wounds

Wounds with yet no cure

Wounds with very thin covering

Our resolve

Thinks about the future only.

Creates a security of a no-go zone

Doctors can heal the wounds permanently

With no possible trace based on the type of revenge used

Our resolve

Let's us know that we are healed

We are better than we will ever know

Will allow us to testify for us

Our resolve

Heals and Thrives us so, we move on"

"What choice is there

None,

No time to think

No time to regroup

No time to waste

Life progresses every minute

So you must lead your life."

Psalm 85:10

"Steadfast love and faithfulness meet; righteousness and peace kiss each other."

Chapter Four

Divorce is the One, if You are Not

It is always a struggle, for divorce is a change that must occur. To some it brings peace and freedom. Divorce creates so many thoughts in your mind, you are scared, you do not want to start over, yet you are so miserable. And suddenly you gain the strength to claim your life and your space back. I had to see divorce as a growth from one level to the next and wanted it badly.

"But my love for a drinking glass, let's me know that if it falls, it breaks, and then I am weakened. Will the break be temporary or permanent? Can the break ever be mended? I think not."

"Walking,

Walk when you can

Walk alone if you must

Walk starts with a stand

I am balanced in my stand as I walk

I stand, I walk, I crawl, I roll, it did not change the choice.

It was clear, stand up and walk out."

"Losses, may the losses I have now, be uncountable like the love to come."

"The loneliest person is sleep, no friends, no enemies... no one to explain your joy or sadness. No one to hurt or help, sleep works alone with no remorse."

"Love, is there such thing? Easily you fall in, easily you fall out."

"There's no such thing as, "I will be by your side forever, because forever is not constant."

"Stand still when there is nothing left to do, then run, walk or crawl."

"Some bones are best left buried."

"Years don't count when peace is being pursued."

"My eyes:

Read them please....

-messages in how they look

-messages in how they open

-messages in how they close

-messages in the tears that flow

-messages in the dryness

My eyes tell their own story of how I am coping and surviving, I respect the stories in my eyes."

"It's yes, I will marry you, not yes, I will have your children."

"Some tears are so silent, they leave you speechless, crying aloud helps."

"I will cry for yesterday, because I am drying my tears today, and when tomorrow comes, my smile will surface with no evidence of tears."

"You are always stronger than your pains."

"May the scars and wounds I have, start a new beginning as they heal."

"Once you've identified your headaches and what caused them, walk and don't look back."

"Escape. Where to? How far?"

Avoidance:

"To accept is to avoid."

"To avoid is to accept."

"Another day of yesterday's struggles, Let's go."

"Time, is what one thinks they have but really don't."

"Waiting, On what? For what? The right time? Not yet? Says who? Wait for nothing. Time moves by the second. Change is constant but varies."

"............. seems farfetched, but I sense my healing will start from your listening."

"You want to share bi/etterness, you'll see the bi/etterment, for I am better."

"Trapped but not afraid of what lies ahead."

"Thorns are like struggles, they hurt, they leave you in shock sometimes, but they are temporary and can be removed with no trace."

"Divorce is Life, Live it well."

"My history will never be my past; it will remain my present and build my future."

"I am Broken yet unbroken in my future."

"Don't worry about convincing people on the choices you make in your life."

"May your present life take no prisoners from our past life."

"An Unexpected bridge,

Do I Panic

Do I cry

Do I give up

No, I take a breath and cross

A bridge is not permanent, its temporary."

Matthew 5:31

"And I say to you, whoever divorces his wife, let him give her a certificate of divorce."

Chapter Five

Singles Are Worth More Than Doubles

So suddenly it dawns on me, I am single again, I take it all in, and allow the air to hit my face and make smooth the rough spots. I want nothing or no one in that moment of realization, except all I need now is to find myself first. I found me; I reintroduce myself to the world I would love to have. I allowed my mind space to connect to a person that will bring me nothing but peace, a person that will fit in that space with me, and in our space. I want to ensure that every moment is memorable and capture beautiful memories to share them with the world. The growth from divorce allowed me to see the peace to live and love freely with no barriers.

"Our soul connects because my heart only beats in my Soul."

"Your mind is your best friend. It keeps all your secrets."

"No one can take what you own, what belongs to you or knows you as the owner."

"Some thoughts are mind deep...Lips don't taste them."

"There are messages in flowers. Read them."

"My yesterday ended a while ago, I am already in my tomorrow, as living today is separate."

"One day, we'll meet and start our journey, A journey we both need. A journey of the minds. A journey of peace. A journey with each day's agenda where we would matter the most."

"My thoughts scare and excite me at the same time."

"My soul wants to trust you because of our connection, but my mind reminds me to be cautious."

"Find a partner that compliments your energy."

"In my silence, I think more."

"My heart runs ahead of me sometimes."

"Distance and waiting defines your destiny. So, I'll take a few steps behind and wait on you as you step forward. Our destiny awaits us."

"Healing can be messy, but the end is powerful."

"Love must be- Bold & Bald.

In her, Boldness there is no fear...

In her, Baldness she needs no validation."

Future

"Future, where are you, what will you be like, Should I be afraid of the unknown, Do I have control of tomorrow?"

"Future, no matter what you hold, I await you wholeheartedly, I embrace your ups and downs, I am not ready for your challenges, but will step in boldly and fiercely."

"Future, I welcome all of you."

"My goal in life, is not the same as my purpose in life. Yet I need them both for Survival."

"Waiting isn't:

An easy thing to do
An assurance of getting your desires."
"Really time limiting, or is it?"

It is:

Best to wait for the right one
Best to learn how to love while waiting.
To help you prepare for tomorrow."

But:

"To wait is golden and most assuring."
"Waiting shows patience and genuineness
because I am waiting for you. I'll wait."

"When strength is the only thing you know,
Life is always lived."

"My mind:

Some days I fight in my mind, other days I am at ease
My mind can be on earth, in heaven and in hell
Control your mind, and don't let it control you."

"Make sure your stress shows you off as stronger."

Psalm 147: 3

"He heals the brokenhearted and binds up all their wounds."

Chapter Six

Friendships Grow You

There are times in life, where great friendships will allow help to increase your sense of belonging and purpose. There are friends who stand by you no matter what your situation is, they are always there. Be sure to have friends who will also caution you when you do wrong.

"A problem shared, is half solved."

"I believe in connections, it brings respect, Not love."

"I celebrate you and our space. I appreciate your genuine spirit and our freedom of expressions. I encourage silence be it independent or individualistic."

"If friendship is your weakest point, then you are the strongest person in the world."

"Gripping my Grapes"

They came clusters, they came single
Some loose or some strong
In clusters we stick together

Clusters or Single

It feels the same.
The peel is smooth and soft

Clusters or Single

Chew on it or suck on it
The feel is the same at times

Clusters or Single

A grape should be moist and tender
With no roughness in sight

Cluster or Single

Grip firmly on to your grapes
And if your hold is loose, it means No Security

Faces Tell:

Sad Stories
Happy Stories
Angry Stories
A face makes faces
A face can control faces
A face tells stories
Control your face
"When folks walk with you up, don't forget them."

"I Want You"

Cannot deny I want you
Cannot deny that I trust you
Cannot deny I have fallen for you
Cannot deny the peace you bring
But I need to know WE want this
I need to know WE trust this
I need to know WE can depend on US
So, let me ask you
Will you respect me?
Will I be your closest friend?
Will you be you and I be me."

"Make every connection worth it."

"Suddenly there are witnesses to your options, those who you thought had no options."

Philippians 2:3

"Do nothing Out of selfish ambition or vain conceit, Rather in humility value others above yourselves."

Chapter Seven

Peace Be with You

And after all the things you go through, your soul will acknowledge peace, yes peace at last, to live freely and boldly. Peace can only be measured by the one who has it, that peace is way bigger and more important than any sadness.

"Smiling and falling asleep."

"My peace, I daydreamed of my peace when would my peace be appearing. Then it happened to me instantly, I acknowledged peace at last."

"A new feeling: My peace, At last."

"Identify the colors of your scars, and dress them up with strength that shines them."

"My soul's peace was not bought, it was not given, it was not shared or divided. It was achieved."

"Persist to remain resilient."

"I need to be careful of my space and make sure you understand who owns it."

"I matter to me."

"Invited guest, please don't overstay your welcome, acknowledge who you are, where you are, how you got here, and enjoy the invite."

"My peace is your peace."

"Being patient, makes life easy, there's a time for everything."

"You've made me realize that it's neither a person, nor a thing, but #MyPeace is an entitlement given to me."

"Thank you for knowing that love is like finding peace for one's soul."

"Smile, a coverup of what's deep within, it could be deceiving, but if you must for a moment, smile anyway."

"The peace your soul needs, your soul knows."

"Peace,

In a situation
In a person
In a thing
In your moments
In your life
Knowing and finding your peace is important."

"My dream, my reality, my tomorrow, I choose me over everything else, I vow to revenge after nothing."

"Together, we will find peace with each passing moment of our time. The peace we discovered, will solidify with what initiated our connection."

"No rush. You are my peace. No one can compare."

"Peace. Eliminates the anger, and gives you joy."

"My happiness, My Success."

"Do good without planning, it's appreciated the most."

"Not asking for your peace, I just need you to respect my peace."

"My peace, my mirror, I see only my peace."

Jude 1:2

"May mercy, peace and love be multiplied in you."

Chapter Eight

Loving Again, And Blessing God for the Truth of Life

Oh yes, there must be love again, the scars, the bruises, the skin tears, the bumps, and the hematomas, must be healed so that your path is set straight, and you have a protection plan in place that will deny reoccurrences. No need to rush, take your time, set your pace, and proceed expeditiously.

"Chosen as strange as it may be to you, I've chosen you for me. I want nothing more in my space, and I want no one else in my corner. I have chosen you."

"Keep forging ahead; As I remember, looking back hinders one's peace to continue, Love Again."

"Sometimes I want you to see my inner peace, the peace you've help me arrived at, with no stress at all."

"A safe space lets you know you're never alone."

"One thing on my mind. I am determined to Love you. No matter what, whether it's in days or years. My soul wants to acknowledge you as it's boss."

"The person that respects your soul must influence your Mind, Body and Soul."

"Don't fine a Soul Mate, find a Mate that respects your Soul."

"Some connections are coincidental, but they are real."

"My Coffee, Smooth, Creamy, and Caramel looking. Every drop lingering like the drop before. Beautiful in taste and appearance. Appreciating the ambience and aroma. Taste depending on my preference. Loving every drop of my coffee."

"My Story may not be what you want to hear, but it's my story. I'll tell it anyway."

"Connection, Friendship, Love, All in one person"

"Walking out of yesterday. Living today for tomorrow."

"Crying"
Rejuvenates peace of mind

Crying
May drown and uplift you

Crying
It is an Acknowledgment of my strength

Crying
An expression of inner feeling."

"At times in life, you must be the only Matter."

"Laughter is good news."

"My eyes are open, not only to see, but it validates life."

"Love is easy when it's right."

"Wait for who you Love."

"Love sees growth not stagnation."

"Being in your own center, is the best thing ever. Crushing on me."

Romans 13:8

"Owe no one anything, except to each other, for the one who loves another has fulfilled the law."

Acknowledgement

I respect every connection from birth till now for giving me a story to tell. I appreciate you and the lessons you taught me. To those of you who encouraged me to tell my story, so that others can be encouraged. I say, "You saw in me, what I did not see." and I remain grateful to each of you.

Mrs. Effua McGowan, thank you for always influencing and challenging me to achieve more.

Habakkuk 2: 3

"The Vision awaits an appointed time, though it lingers, wait it will certainly come without delay."

About the Author

Miss Glendy Jane Junius

Glendy Junius is a Mother and has been a Passionate Nurse for more than 22 years. Glendy was born on June 13, 1969, in Liberia, Grand Bassa County, West Africa. Glendy now lives in Virginia with her Mother Ethel, and 5 Children. In her spare time, she browses Social Media, listens to music, sings, writes quotes, decorates, and make floral arrangements. She is a part of, and participates in many Charity organizations, working on giving back to her home country and People of Liberia.

Glendy is a graduate of the University of Liberia, with a Bachelor's Degree in Business Administration, and also holds a Bachelor's of Science Degree in Nursing from Phoenix University.

www.ingramcontent.com/pod-product-compliance
Lightning Source LLC
Chambersburg PA
CBHW071501160426
43195CB00013B/2175